HOW
SHE
HEALS

poems

Shelly M. Smith

20 🐴 16
Brown Horse Press

To Mandy,
Hope you find
something in here
you like!
Shelly

Printed in the United States of America

First Printing, 2016

ISBN: 978-0-9982101-0-0

Brown Horse Press
P.O. Box 1233
Pickens, SC 29671

brownhorsepress@gmail.com

Cover photo and design by Shelly M. Smith.
Cover formatting by Elizabeth Fox Brewer.
Interior design and formatting by Elizabeth Fox Brewer.
Editing and proofing by Davis Horner.

For Mom and Dad

AUTHOR'S NOTE

There are six poems in this book written entirely in italics. These poems came to me during prayer/meditation. I sometimes refer to them as coming from "The Voice."

As for who or what the "voice" is, I'll leave to you to decide.

CONTENTS

HOW SHE HEALS

MY BACKYARD

Oh that others could know what they're missing,
with their busyness
and cell phones
and traffic,

and the constant pull
of what needs to happen next.

If only they could know
the way of Silence –

except for the chirping chaos
of backyard birds –
some close, others farther away,

and how they call us to stop.
And wait.

And hear within their disparate songs
and within the space between their songs,

the Truth –

as a Presence

that waits

wanting only to fulfill Itself

through our seemingly separate bodies

as It does the birds.

WHEN YOU LIVE ALONE

When you live alone
in the country,
with only the animals
and the moon
to keep you company,

you become someone different
from who you thought you were –
something less identified
as human –
as different or separate
from the plants and the wild things
that have become your friends.

Like the daisies who died today –
cut by the mower,
and I felt so sad,

for when I walked past the other day
they were beautiful,
looking down on them
from five feet above,

and yet,

moments later,

lying next to them,

my face close to theirs,

they were family

all of a sudden –

equals

not underlings.

And so I cried

when I found them,

shredded in the grass,

with their shredded friends.

And I think how strange it is,

that such a subtle shift

in my perspective meant

that I was no longer

an observer of nature,

but Nature

Herself.

TRUST

When life happens
and you don't know what to do
you can always do nothing
and see what happens.

For the God that's in you
always knows the way.

What you call real
is only a story,
but the God that's in you
is the only story that's true.

Don't misunderstand me,
I'm not into idol worship –
what you tend to glorify
is not God to me at all.
And indolence is never
an act of faith.

But when you know

really know

you are that which created you,

you cease *trying* to do

you cease *trying* to be

you cease *trying* to make

anything else happen, at all,

and you rest in quiet knowing

as That,

which you are.

THE COYOTE

Were you injured?

Were you lost?

Unafraid you seemed,

when you saw me and mine

on that parcel of land

I think I own

but in fact belongs to you

and all your brethren.

Time waited,

as we stared at one another.

You know me,

as one to be wary of.

Best that I not find you out –

your secret ways

and your secret life.

Hated by some,

hunted by others.

But to me,

you are a masterpiece.

For as we stare I remember

things I almost forgot,

like what it means to be free,

what it means to be wild.

MY EVENING WALK

In the fading orange glow
of a sun already set,
I walk through David's pasture
like I've done a thousand times before.

I greet each cow silently
apologetically
and with a little shame –
for we both know their purpose here.
It's only a matter of time.

But how drab would this world be –
without cows
and their sweet cow babies
scampering playfully
on a warm spring night?

And then,
the bright yellow bi-plane
flies directly overhead –
so low –

so low I can almost see its student pilot

as he heads straight for orange sky.

And as I turn to wave

my full-armed wave

with such child-like joy,

he gently tips his wings

to wave right back.

And I practically skip the whole way home –

thinking how lucky I am

to live next door

to David's pasture.

JUST AFTER DUSK

When darkness comes
it settles.
And crickets sing.

It's my favorite time –
the gray time,

when everything waits
suspended,

for something clear and startling,
but it never comes.

Only the quiet,

and the endless hum of crickets
and far-off traffic,

and a mystery within a pause
of nothingness,

'til light shines his face
again.

SIMPLY ME

I am a girl
who loves God
who loves her home in the mountains
and everything wild.

I am not special
I am not especially smart
but I love what I love
and that'll have to be enough.

I'd hoped that one day I'd be famous,
that someone powerful might see
some great gift
I have to share.

But alas I am simply me –
waiting
and wondering
and writing
my way home.

BUDDHA COWS

Even the black ones look speckled,

lying under

the budding oak tree

as the midday sun

filters down

from overhead.

So peacefully they wait,

silently

so quietly

as if in trance;

completely with themselves,

completely with each other,

and I wonder,

"Don't they know their fate?"

Some say that they are stupid,

that this can't possibly be so.

But if stupid means not knowing

and not fretting,

so contentedly in the now,

then I wish that I could be

as stupid

as a cow.

GRACE

I don't know what makes me worthy
of this great and remarkable life –
what I did or didn't do
to deserve such love.

I only know that somehow
God found a way,
through the tenseness and armor
of my self-defended heart,

to bestow me with perfection
in this less than perfect world,

for this less than perfect girl.

THE NATURE OF TRUTH

You must know there is a place
beyond what you see
beyond what you can imagine,
with your mind full of constructs
and beliefs
about what is real.

The mind thinks it knows
but it cannot.

The Truth can only be felt –
perhaps with your heart,
but always through
the relinquishment
of the trappings
of what you think of as solid,
about yourself
and about the world.

For the Truth cannot be defended,
it cannot be proved.

Yet it is palpably, interminably alive,
pulsating within the spaces
of what you think of
as life.

SELF-PORTRAIT

My way is strange
to those who know not
the call of the Lord.
For in quiet he comes –
subtly, softly,

seeking to fulfill
and make himself known
within this hardened shell

which braces –
for no other reason
that I can tell,
except habit.

There is a way to write
that paints a picture,
for those who cannot see,

but I tell you,
I am not a picture painter

or a songbird

or a muse.

I am a girl

who lies in the grass

who waits in the silence

who hears nothing and everything,

all at the same time.

WHAT THE DAISIES TAUGHT ME

I had admired them for weeks –
the island patch of daisies
in the middle of the pasture
that I walk through each day
to check on the horses.

They looked like a family,
or a town –
a little community all their own,

their happy faces
gathered together
amidst the tall grass
and an odd thistle or two.

But I forgot to tell the mower guy
not to cut them when he came today.

Only half are standing now –
in shock it seems to me.
The other half shredded –

half the community gone.

And I think about the terrible things
that have happened to me
and to other people

and a wise man who once said,

It's not personal.
It's not personal.

THE FENDER BENDER

Over a half dozen people
on the side of the road
blue lights flashing
no one hurt – thank goodness.

I notice the mix of people –
mostly smiling and talking
kindly
with each other,

and I notice the cars –
a shiny new Lexus
a farmer's rusty old truck
and everything in-between,

but each with a dent
or a crumpled tailgate.

And I think about the people –
each with dents and stories of their own –
and how Life can level the playing field.

For in this one brief moment

it's not the cars that matter

or the money that bought them,

but the gestures of compassion

and smiles between strangers

as they each forgive each other

for being human.

A TALE OF ROMANTIC LOVE

My quest for the *Other*
led me to you.
You filled His space perfectly –
or so I thought.

I wanted you to be
and so you were,
but neither of us realized
the toll it would take.

You got tired
and I was shocked,
devastated,
when the dream,
the illusion,
finally died.

All that I thought was true
about this "ultimate love"
shattered.

For you

are not Him.

He

is me.

And that is bigger

and freer

and fuller

than I ever imagined.

My search for the *Other*

has ended

with my Self.

MY FORMER SELF
(A Menopause Poem)

I miss her –

the one who knew it all,

who never had a doubt,

who always had a point to prove.

Moxie.

Fire!

She might have been scared

but she'd never tell –

the girl who always *always*

got back on the horse that threw her.

Oh, I do miss her.

What a friendly illusion she was –

full of vim and vigor.

But life came crashing down –

crash after crash.

And then she saw
that it wasn't real –
that *she*
wasn't real.

And then she died and I realized . . .

she didn't know much
after all.

TRYING HARD TO BE NORMAL

I turn on the TV
as I wash the dishes
trying to be
like a regular person –
not confused by reality.
(Whose?)

It's midday.
And the crickets are singing
their autumn death song
and I can hardly attend
to the dishes and things –

pulled as I am
to a world that feels safe
where they patiently wait,

their high-pitched humming saying:
Come, we have what you need!

And I feel myself there
and I feel myself here

as I go back to the dishes

and the stupid TV

and to this human body

I'm trying to call home.

THE KNOWN WAY

All this petty worry
about money
and business

while the backyard birds sing happily,
unconcerned,
sharing their gifts of song
without ego
or agenda,
except for the sheer and simple joy
of being themselves.

And I think about what Jesus said
about the birds
and about the Father,

and why it's so hard for me to believe,
that I'm cared for
and that I'm worthy.

The least of these, he said.

But my mind cannot conceive it.

So it goes back to what's familiar –

chasing demons

I cannot see.

ENOUGH

The bright yellow birds
hopping and pecking
at the feeder
do not wonder,
"Am I enough?"

The horses –
their shiny coats
glaring
under a midday sun
do not wonder,
"Am I enough?"

But me,
exhausted and spent
from years of trying
and efforting
and hoping to prove
something,

still wonders,
"Am I enough?"

THE GIFT OF ADRENAL FATIGUE

When you're too tired to think,
when you're too tired to care,
your perspective changes.

And you realize
that you could have
felt this way
all along.

And you realize
that all the struggling
and effort,
to make things happen,
to make yourself feel safe,

was just that –
struggling.

And your sweet precious body
couldn't take it anymore.
So it said, *Enough*.

We're done.

This is not the way.

For that which you seek
is not in the doing,
or some future event.

But in the still quiet spaces
of your own
exhausted heart.

DEARLY DEPARTED

I'm off to a funeral.
Striving died today,
along with her friends
Perfectionist
and Hustle.

They overdosed
on the same drug –
a form of adrenaline
which promised
approval
and recognition
finally
once and for all.

I'm not sad to see them go –
not really,
for they'd suffered
for so long.

And it was painful to watch

their misguided efforts –
grasping for something
that just wasn't there.

And now they're at peace –

resting in the arms
of what they wanted
all along.

EGO DEATH

There is a peace which follows
death –
of a certain kind.

The kind which follows
exhaustion –
when you realize
that who you thought you were
and what you thought you wanted

was not who you were
or what you wanted at all.

And all the striving
and straining
of trying to prove your worth,
your godliness,
through culture-bound constraints
becomes empty and shallow.

And you know what you have to do . . .

surrender –

let your foot off the brake

and let life do

what life is bound to do

to you

and to everybody –

knowing that control

is only an illusion

without which

you are free.

THE WILD SECRET

I don't know what I did
to deserve such fate –
a miracle really –
that one so wounded
and one so defended
could find herself held
in the arms
of such a God-filled space.

And I wonder about the purpose
for those who have not
their heart's desire,

who struggle and weep
and feel so unworthy.
I wish that I could tell them,

I know so much about what you feel
and how it hurts
when you don't know
this wild secret that you're carrying –

that you are made in the image
of the One who sent you,
and like it or not,
you are entirely

enough.

LAST NIGHT'S PRAYER

Give me a way, I asked,
to be in this world
without striving or effort.

Like the flowers of the field
through which You breathe
into blossom every spring.

Like the creek which tumbles
over rocks,
persistently onward,

taking with it
sticks and leaves

who helplessly happily
surrender to its flow.

Make me as pure
as Your creatures and plants,
who seek to be

no more

or less

than what You created them to be.

May I be so obedient.

May I be so free.

REAL POETRY

They say it's work – *real* poetry.
That if it comes too easily
it must not be,
worthy of the same name,
which others sweat
and labor over.

But I don't know if I believe,
that it has to be hard to count.
For what is hard about breathing
and listening,
for that which you are,
to speak?

PAYING ATTENTION

Have you ever noticed
how the setting sun
casts a burnt-orange glow
into the trees,
or onto buildings where you live?

And have you ever noticed
how a Sunday
can make you feel so peaceful,
or even lazy,
and by evening,
a little blue?

And have you ever noticed
a tight pinch in your chest,
or a fluttering in your gut,
and how you quickly turn your attention
to something to distract you?

But most importantly of all,
have you ever noticed

the one who is noticing,

and stopped to wonder

who that is?

I SEE YOU

Poems aren't always pretty.
Sometimes they kick your ass –
like the ones that remind you that
you're not alone but you are,
that you're eternal but you're not.

This world it seems
is full of contradictions.
But contradictions are only
our failure to see
our lives and this world
through the eyes of,

the Seer.

Instead we tend
to see through the eyes
of one who sees only,
what fits in a box
of this or that.

But the problem with boxes is –

they tend to be small

and manageable

and separate.

And you dear friend,

are not.

GOOD ENOUGH POETRY

A mockingbird woke me this morning,
and I'm glad he didn't stop to think
about how it might sound –
what order his notes
or phrasing
should go in.

For there was no plan –
it wasn't contrived.
He was simply being
what he was made to be –
himself.

And it didn't cross my mind
to offer my critique
or analysis of
his art.

And I think how strange it is
that we strive for perfection
in ourselves and in others,

when Perfection is here
in the mockingbird's song

and in feeble attempts
to put words
on a page.

NO ORDINARY LOVER

Take me with you I will go
wherever you lead –
my trusted lover and friend.

For you know me by name
and each hair on my head
as if I were more precious to you,

more valuable,
than anyone else.
But I know it's not true.

I know you love the others
just the same.
But do they love you as I do?

Do their hearts beat as mine does,
when I lie awake
in the grass

in the soft sweet bed

it seems you made

just for me?

HORSES

As Family

I wish I could tell you
what it's like
to be heard without speaking,

to be understood,
without even knowing
what you yourself
are thinking,
or feeling.

And to know that you're not judged,
but forgiven,

over and over
again,

for being so clumsy
and disconnected
from who you are,

by those who have never

forgotten.

Myself As Horse (1)

To feel the shame
of not belonging,

the frustration when
they cannot see
the things that you see
that aren't there,

or the things that you hear
that can only be heard
by other creatures
like you,

who aren't human,
but are no less intelligent
and no less worthy –
just different.

Myself As Horse (2)

Forgive me if I stumble
when I try to express,
with human words,
that which is bigger
than words.

Language is limited.
It doesn't convey
a sense or a feeling,
unless it's through music
or poetry –

my latest attempt
to share the Unseen
and feel at home,
among humans.

How They Talk (1)

The twitch of an ear,
the swish of a tail
says everything.

It's fast.

It's clear.

It's honest.

No need for strings

of words,

held in a brain,

prolonging a feeling

long after it's passed,

in order to explain

to those who need words,

because they don't talk

with feelings.

How They Talk (2)

Body language they say –

the humans who observe

and think they've decoded

a language,

they'll never understand.

For what's put into words

has already passed,

for a creature who speaks

whole pages

in seconds.

The Great Ones

What *real* horse whisperers know,

is that they'll never know

everything there is to know

about that which is

unknowable.

And therein lies

their genius –

as humans whose arrogance

is held in check

by a reverent respect

for that which is more

in tune and connected

than they are.

ME AND BROWN

A football field away, at least
from the house to her shed,
where she stands meditating
or dozing
as she often does.

And me
at the kitchen window
seeing her and smiling, when
UP
snaps her head,

as she looks at me –
right at me
as if she can see me
but she can't.
And yet she can *feel* me
looking at her.

And it's happened so often
these last twenty years

that I can't help but laugh
at the scientists who say,

Eureka!
A horse can read body language!
Our important research says so!

God save me from those
who observe
but cannot see,

who are learned
but don't *know,*

what it's like
to be family
with a horse.

POETS' FIRST LUNCH

Just when I think
that it isn't safe,
or worth the trouble,
to share my heart with another . . .
the other comes.

Surprising me
with his depth and compassion,
and willingness –
to hear without fixing
and to mirror without judgment.

I had thought that only
the horses could do that,
but perhaps I was wrong.

Perhaps when one poet
shares her heart with another,
the writing itself makes
a bridge which says:

STAND NAKED HERE.

YOUR JEWEL

Only when one
has plumbed their own depths
can they be comfortable
with yours.

Do not waste your precious
vulnerability,
and the bright jewel within it,

on those who know nothing
of either.

SEEING VERSUS LOOKING

Seeing is not looking.
Seeing is for taking in
the beauty
all around you.

It bypasses the mind
and goes straight to
your heart.

Looking involves pursuit –
of something –
anything,
to satisfy the mind's
hunger for something
it cannot know

until it sees.

SPECIAL BONDS

There are some bonds
you can never replace,
although it's tempting to try,
especially when you're grieving
the loss of a beloved
animal friend

who is taken too soon.
Yet aren't they always?

Some connections are earned
from a time and a place
beyond this one
it seems.

And it's tempting to ask why
this one feels different.

But we're left with a mystery
and our grief
and our love

which seems to go on

forever.

THE GIFT OF GRIEF

Grief,

when given a space to

be grief –

lovingly held

with your own compassion . . .

is a gift.

For it opens you,

to the best of you –

the Great Consoler and

the one who has loved . . .

so deeply.

MUTE FRUSTRATION

There are things I want to say –
things I've wanted to say
for a long time.
But where to begin?

I am told that I saw things
when I was little –
that I pointed and exclaimed,

but I don't remember
what I saw
that the others
could not see,

only the seething
indignant
frustration,

in trying to explain
the inexplicable.

I feel it still.

LITTLE FINCH

Amidst the steel cables

and cross braces

she sings.

She sings her heart out.

A trilling melodious sound

not far

over my head

where I stand in line

at Lowe's

with the flowers

and bags of mulch

and it's hot,

and the computer is down

and everyone sighs

as the line keeps growing,

and nobody notices

the tiny angel

with her powerful song –

except me.

SUMMER AND THE SOUTHERN GIRL

Some say it's too hot
and make life inside
their climate-controlled
houses and cars.

I can't say that I blame them,
especially if
they live within concrete
and asphalt
and steel,

and don't have the luxury
of a great oak who
offers protection
from the high sun's heat,
and seems to stir
whatever air
is moving
at all.

Just give me a swing

which dangles beneath
layers and layers
of leafy barked arms,

and I will make peace
with the heat.

As my ancestors did –
as the horses do.

For I would rather be hot
than for one moment feel separate

from what I love
where I came from
and who I am.

TROUBLE WITH TIME

I'm always running late.
I have trouble with time.
It's not that I can't tell it –
it's just that I don't accept it
as important as honoring that

Brown wants to stand
with me today
at the open gate,
leading back to her pasture
after her breakfast.

And I can't and I won't tell her no.

And if you knew her like I did
you'd understand
what an honor it is
to be chosen,
over her friends,
considering that I'm
only human
after all.

And sometimes the breeze
stirs the oak trees just right
and I'm distracted
by a mischief
I can feel
but can't prove.

It's the same with the hummers
and blue jays and tits,
their fluttering busyness,
zooming this way and that,
is far more enchanting
than my own
human life.

So I find myself lost
in a world that's not mine.
And now you know why
I have trouble
with time.

MIDLIFE REFLECTION

I don't know when, *exactly* when, it happened,
that they stopped noticing, stopped staring –
the men who noticed and stared
for so long.

I'm invisible now.

And it seems so strange to me
for I look in the mirror and I see
the same eyes I've always seen
the same person I've always been –
only different.

For now there is a light
that I couldn't see before
of a well-earned knowing
and a well-lived life.

And I take comfort in the fact
that even if, one day, I'm tucked away
in some awful place
with other invisible people,

I have only to look
at my own reflection to see
the one who showed up
who faced her demons,

and helped others
do the same.

CREEK THERAPY

It's one thing to sit
and hear their stories.

It's another to teach them
some tools,
to help them feel better
about themselves,
and about their feelings.

But there's something else that happens
that's harder to explain
in the space
between the words.

Some call it magic,
others call it God,
but we know it when we feel it

and we'll stop –
with a mutual unspoken agreement
and wait –
fully expecting to hear

a voice in the breeze

or as if
the *tinkle tinkle* of the creek

will rise

and morph into a song
a message
or a prayer.

LITTLE BLACK SNAKE

I lingered
a little longer
on the bridge
over the creek

knowing there was a reason
but not sure what,

when I saw the tips
of the tall grass moving
barely,
down next to the water,
and I watched

waiting for you to show yourself –
the one I felt
watching me.

And you cautiously slithered
barely into view
in the shadows beneath the grass –

so polite and respectful of my

space,

that I couldn't imagine

who would kill you

and why –

one so gentle

and sensitive

as you.

HOW SHE HEALS

It has saved me more than once –
this example that she gives
of life renewing life.

For every winter she dies,
(or so it seems),
with her bare branches and brown grass
and the darkness that settles
as if to stay, forever.

And I wait with her in the dark
and I wonder if we're done,
and if the silent grayness
and sleep,
are the new normal.

Then quietly she rouses –
a little here
a little there
and I wake up slowly with her,

in utter amazement, once again

on seeing what was growing

while it seemed

that we were sleeping.

WAITING WORSHIP

I will not seek Thee. No.
For within my seeking lie
my opinions,
about who You are
and what You can do for me.

Instead I will wait –
as the sheep waits for
her shepherd,

allowing myself
to be surprised

by the many ways
You find me.

PROSPERITY

I must make peace with prosperity.
Knowing that I, am one of the fortunate
who, for reasons not of my own making,
has plenty.

And I don't know why it should be so,
when there are others who suffer
who can't get a break. And we tend to
soften our guilt with a judgment saying,
it must be karma, or worse yet, laziness.

I've heard some horrible stories, as one who is paid
to hear others' pain, and I can tell you
there are no good reasons, as mentioned above –

only the bitter discrepancies that Jesus himself
acknowledged then said: *Be grateful. Be grateful.*
Be glad.

WHAT THE VOICE SAID

I want you to tell them
that all is well.
I want you to say that
there is nothing they can do
to un-earn my love.

For my love is Love.
It doesn't falter,
it doesn't wane.

It's not like the wind,
that blows here or there –
blessing some,
depriving others.

It is instead,
the very substance of air –
not defined by its action
or lack thereof,
but within and beyond both,
having no judgment,

about either.

I would no more seek to judge you,
for this action or that,
anymore than I would judge

the wind –
for blowing
or not.

For I am the wind.

And I am you.

HEALER HEAL THYSELF

Tenderly I hold her. Up all night with a
gastric disturbance of explosive proportions
which made her wonder why she drank
the slimy potion, intended to heal
the fist of an organ, which seems to be falling
down on the job – a little.

But poison as medicine is not new to her.

How grateful she feels, to carry the snake
as totem inside her, who takes great delight
in transforming a chemical, of any kind:
anger into passion, fear into humility,
grief into love, and so on.

And many a night
I've lain awake beside her
holding her hand –

the one so determined
to feel and heal
her way through life.

A NATION OF ADDICTS

You say you're not addicted?

What do you miss

when you sit

alone

in the silence,

with only yourself

and your breath

for company?

ANIMAL CRUELTY

Our treatment of those

not human

is ghastly.

I cannot conceive

of the mind who treats

another of God's

like a thing.

I can only surmise

that he sees Him as

a king on a throne

who he's trying to emulate.

It's a metaphor you dumbass!

HUMAN ARROGANCE

You think yourself superior as
you go through your days,
believing you are
above those creatures
who perish,

under your foot
of careless disregard,
as you climb your way,
to the top
of the heap.

But from where I sit,
you know nothing
of greatness.

For even the ant
works for the whole.

HER ANGER

Her anger scares her.
Oh sure, she can spew it
or spit it

like a snake who slithers
undetected until
it strikes

at an unsuspecting offhand comment
made by a man
or a child she loves.

But the spirit of the snake isn't mean –
just frustrated by
the confining container created
by her fear
of its power,

to challenge how she sees herself
and who she's supposed to be.

IT SKIPS A GENERATION

All this beauty, and all that I can think of is
how much there is to do and
how little I have done and
what a sorry excuse of
a human-accomplisher I am.

And the whole thing makes me tired
when I consider all the repairs
and the mowing and the tending
which never ends and yet,

somehow it gets done –
enough of it anyway to
satisfy the critic – my father
inside my head –
for long enough to wait,
for a poem
or two.

So with a nod toward his father,
the unsuccessful dreamer,

I gaze out to the mountain for
a dose of inspiration thinking,

*Don't worry PaPa. I'll take it
from here.*

THE POTTER SPEAKS

Fall safely into My arms
and let yourself rest
as I watch over you,
and admire the features
I know as My own,

as I recollect every overcoming
and struggle
we shared – together.

For every potter knows
the clay is not his slave,
but his cherished inspiration
of Himself as

Creator.

DEAR CREATOR

Did I come to you first as a feeling?
A spark of quiet something that
you knew to pause and wait for?
And did you smile when you felt me
bearing down on you
knowing what was coming
a delicious tension brewing?
And did you watch with patient joy
as the first fragments of me
peeped shyly into view?
And did your heart expand with privileged pride
as who I came to be
unfolded, before your eyes?

I'm only asking this because

writing poetry
is like that.

BROWN

So often she will stand transfixed
not with alarm, but with concern
and I'll follow her gaze
inevitably to see
a hawk's great swooping
down

on a terrified chicken,
or a baby goat whose head is stuck
in his human's hog-wire fence,
bawling as a newborn babe
inconsolable.

And it gives me cause to wonder
whatever else she sees
and how she reconciles
her helpless impotent concern
for innocent others
around our home.

I wish she could teach me how.

THE DOE

So sorry to disturb you Miss,

but you didn't have to snort

your indignant disapproval and

your warning to the others.

It's our pasture too!

But I will give you this:

I'll wager that you know

each and every blade of grass,

and every errant weed,

as you know each tawny hair

on your warily twitching hide,

and I'll bet this pastured hill

with its teeming green-lit life,

breathes itself through you

as the Beloved breathes through me.

The only difference is

you have never

thought otherwise.

ANOTHER DAY

that I wish
that I didn't have to speak
to a single soul –
afraid that I might miss

something real and important,
within the quiet lovely character
of the trees and the bees
and the still humid
summer air –

about me
and about the world
and my place in it.

There's a dream
that I gave up on
long ago –

another human
to sit with me

and hear

what I hear

together

saying nothing.

WHAT ELSE THE VOICE SAID

1.

My child!
My child!

If you only knew
how free you were

you would dance,
all of your days

and sing,
with full-throated praise

the glory of yourself
as Me.

You are the flute for My fluting
and its air which sings.

Do you think that I would stop you
from being these things?

2.

My nourishment is free
and available to all.

It matters not to Me
whether you drink

a thimble-full
or an ocean's share,

but one day you will drink freely,

knowing it is My
great pleasure,

to give you the Kingdom.

3.

There is only this –
the Breath.

As I fill you
you feed Me,

returning Me
to more of Me.

It's all I ask.

LOVE'S REQUEST

Let me write you my Beloved!

Let me ride you as
the surfer rides his wave.

For the character of your shape
allows me to express
that of me who

without you

would be lost.

ANNIVERSARY

We sat on the rock
with our feet in the water
just like we did
ten years ago and

remembered that time
and the promises made
and the promises kept
and the ones that were not

and how just like before
we gazed at the water
reflecting the trees and the blue sky above
and ourselves in each other
imagined and true

only this time we're freer
'cause the water is clearer
renewing our vows –
the *non-vows* we call them.

PEACE AND JOY

The title was *Peace* –
the Caring Bridge entry –
written by his wife saying
just this morning he passed.
He was only 59 and
diagnosed not long ago,

and since that time her entries
speak of stents and infection
chemo and appointments –
facts calmly and clearly
conveyed to keep us up to date,

but mostly overshadowed by
her gratitude for friends –
boxes of food delivered
and help with transportation –

and for small reliefs and comforts
and their love for each other.

Like this morning when she told him
how grateful she was for him,
as they shared their favorite memories
in their last hours together,

and told him he'd done well, and
how they would all be fine,
as she read to him some letters
and played his favorite waltzes.

And in closing this last entry
she expressed in typical fashion,
her gratitude for all of us as
"we get through this together."

And yet it's me who should feel grateful –
split open and made speechless
by words made soft by cancer and
a widow whose name is . . . *Joy*.

WHAT I'LL SAY
WHEN I GET TO HEAVEN

If I had known

what was waiting

here,

on the other side,

I would have run toward every fear,

hungry

for its freedom.

I would have shed

the heavy armor

of self-conscious

self-protection,

and cast it

into the pit

with the other costumes

that I wore.

And flung

my wild heart open

at every

single thing,

and danced naked

while singing,

You cannot die!

It's just a dream!

ACKNOWLEDGMENTS

I would like to thank the following people: Jana Sains, Elizabeth Fox Brewer, Jennie Wakefield, Scott Henderson, Jim Hutcheson, Kim Gardner-Midgett, Suzie Medders, Jim Ross, David Hendricks, Joy Hughes, Laura Garren, James King, Sonja Neely, Davis and Kathleen Horner, and the lovely souls at Unity Church Clemson/Anderson, SC, and the Friends Quaker Meeting in Greenville, SC.

I would also like to express my deep love and appreciation for my spiritual life partner, Steve Midgett, who has always seen me and believed in me. His integrity and tireless commitment to living the creative life is an example to us all.

Lastly, I want to express my gratitude for my beloved horse family and the wild creatures who share the magical property that I call home.

It is my inspiration. It is how God finds me.

ABOUT THE AUTHOR

Shelly M. Smith grew up in Henderson, North Carolina, and has lived her entire life in the South. She has always had an empathic relationship with animals, nature, and humans.

She currently resides in Pickens County, SC, at the edge of the Blue Ridge Mountains, where she conducts workshops and private sessions on her property and by phone. She is a personal growth facilitator and animal intuitive.

Ms. Smith is a Licensed Professional Counselor and Licensed Marriage and Family Therapist.

For more information, please visit: www.shellysmith.org and www.whenanimalstalk.com.

ADDITIONAL COPIES

of this book may be purchased by contacting:

Brown Horse Press
P.O. Box 1233
Pickens, SC 29671

brownhorsepress@gmail.com

or online through Amazon.com.

Kindle version available

December 1, 2016